DISCOVER THE CELTS
AND THE IRON AGE

Everyday Life

MOIRA BUTTERFIELD

W

Franklin Watts
Published in paperback in Great Britain in 2018 by The Watts Publishing Group

Credits
Series Editor: John C. Miles
Series Designer: Jane Hawkins
Picture researcher: Kathy Lockley

Picture credits: Alamy/Sabena Jane Blackbird: 17 Christina Bollen: 9 C.M.Dixon/AAA Collection: 12 James Emmerson/Robert Harding: 27 David Lyons: 10B Werner Forman Archive/Heritage Image Partnership: Titlepage, 6BR, 13, 16, 23, 25T © The Trustees of the British Museum: Cover (Main image), 14 CORBIS/Gideon Mendel/In Pictures: 28 National Museum of Wales: 19 REX/Shutterstock: 21 Shutterstock.com/art_of_sun: Cover donatas1205: Cover Jaime Pharr: 29 Tanarch: 7 TopFoto.co.uk/Topham Picturepoint: 5 Wikipedia/ http://www.numismantica.com: 4 (and throughout book) Jacopo Werther/Andres Rueda: 11 Photo by Helen Etheridge: 15 Photo by Johnbod: 22 Photo by Jorge Royan: 24 Photo by LordHarris at English Wikipedia: 18

Every attempt has been made to clear copyright. Should there be any inadvertent omission please apply to the publisher for rectification.

ISBN 978 1 4451 6203 4

Printed in China

MIX
Paper from responsible sources
FSC® C104740
www.fsc.org

Franklin Watts
An imprint of
Hachette Children's Group
Part of The Watts Publishing Group
Carmelite House
50 Victoria Embankment
London EC4Y 0DZ

An Hachette UK Company
www.hachette.co.uk

www.franklinwatts.co.uk

CONTENTS

ALL ABOUT THE IRON AGE

Life was very different in Britain in the time between 3,000 and 2,000 years ago. Nobody lived in a big city. Nobody spoke English. Nobody even knew how to write. We call this period of history the Iron Age. It came to an end when the ancient Romans invaded in CE 43.

WHY THE IRON AGE?

About 3,000 years ago (roughly around 800 BCE) the Iron Age began when travellers from other parts of Europe brought the secret of making iron to Britain. Before then people used bronze to make their farm tools and weapons, in a time we call the Bronze Age. Iron was cheaper, tougher and quicker to make than bronze.

MEET THE CELTS

At the beginning of the Iron Age, fewer than 1 million people lived in Britain (now there are around 65 million people). They lived in small family groups, farming the land to feed themselves. Most people in northern Europe lived in the same way. We call them all the Celts.

DID THE CELTS LIVE NEAR ME?

The Iron Age Celts lived all over Britain, as far north as the Scottish Islands. Your local museum might have some Iron Age objects found near where you live.

THE BRITONS

Iron Age Celts did not write, but some early visitors wrote about them. A Greek explorer called Pytheas called the locals 'prettani', which may mean 'tattooed people'. The Romans changed the word 'prettani' to Britons, the name we still use today.

FROM THE IRON AGE

Finds dug up from the ground help us to understand more about the Iron Age. This find is one of the most incredible of all – a real Iron Age Briton! He was a human sacrifice killed around 2,000 years ago. You can find out more about him on p22.

Lindow Man's body was put into a peat bog. The chemicals in the soil preserved him. ▼

WHO'S WHO?

Tribal chiefs were the most powerful people in Iron Age times. They were buried with treasures, such as swords and shields. Most ordinary Iron Age Celts were not buried in graves, and all that we know about them comes from things they left behind in the places where they lived.

WARRIORS AND DRUIDS

Iron Age Celts gathered into tribes based in different areas. Bands of loyal warriors kept their tribal chiefs in power and fought other tribes for land or valuable belongings, such as cattle and horses. The chiefs had religious advisors called Druids, who made predictions about the future rather like astrologers do today. The chiefs listened to their advice.

MEET THE WORKERS

Ordinary Celts spent their time doing everyday tasks to feed and clothe themselves and their families. They were kept busy with jobs, such as tending crops, looking after animals, collecting water and weaving wool to make their own clothes. They might have been cremated (burnt) when they died, but we don't know for sure. All we have left from them are bits and pieces from their everyday life, such as fragments of pottery and

This gold coin was made in the late Iron Age, around 2,000 years ago. It is marked with the name of Cunobelin, a powerful leader of the Catuvellauni tribe in southeast England. One side shows a horse and the other shows an ear of corn.

weaving tools. They probably didn't own very much - just the things they needed to survive.

SOME TRIBAL NAMES

When the Romans arrived in Britain they wrote down the names of Iron Age tribes. Here are the names of a few of the tribes in power at the time. They were written down by a Roman geographer called Ptolemy.

Iceni – Eastern England
Dumnonii – Western England
Brigantes – Northern England
Ordovices – North Wales
Caledones – Northern Scotland
Taexali – Northeast Scotland
Epidii – West Scotland
Parisi – Northeast England
Demetae – West Wales
Cantiaci – Southeast England
Catuvellauni – Southeast England

WHICH TRIBE LIVED NEAR ME?

You can go online to see a map of the Iron Age tribes in Britain. There is an Internet link shown on p31.

▲ Some of the tribes of Celtic Britain

WHO LIVED HERE?

Some Iron Age Celts lived in just a few thatched huts grouped together in fields. Others lived in big hill forts guarded by deep ditches and high banks. Some even lived in stone towers. Wherever they lived, people built defences around their homes.

ROUND HUT HOMES

Iron Age Britons lived in roundhouses with pointed thatched roofs. Inside everybody shared one big room, sometimes with farm animals. In Scotland some people lived in crannogs - roundhouses built on platforms jutting out onto lakes. They farmed the land around the lake, but if their enemies arrived they could hide in the crannog.

INSIDE A HILL FORT

During the Iron Age some tribes began to put roundhouses inside big hill forts high up on hilltops, defended by rings of banks and ditches. Inside a hill fort there were homes, crop stores and sometimes religious shrines, too. Hill forts could be seen for miles around and they were a symbol of tribal power. They sent a message to neighbouring tribes - "This land is ours!".

DID CELTS HAVE TOWNS?

At the end of the Iron Age, around 2,000 years ago, some Celts began living in *oppida* - communities with homes built along streets. Oppidum were the very first small towns.

STAYING SAFE

Even the smallest farms would have had a high fence of wooden stakes to keep out enemies and wild animals. In the north-west of Scotland people went even further and built stone towers called brochs, with walls up to 4 m thick. As well as human enemies there were wolves, wild boars and even brown bears in Celtic Britain.

8

FROM THE IRON AGE

This copy of a crannog has been reconstructed on Loch Tay in Scotland. When divers excavated an original crannog in the Loch they found lots of things preserved in the peaty water, including clothing, food and even a butter dish with Iron Age butter in it.

COME INSIDE

Can you imagine living in a roundhouse? It would be warm and cosy but dark and smoky, too. All the things you needed for cooking, eating and sleeping would be dotted around.

ALL IN TOGETHER

A roundhouse had one small door and no windows. The walls were made of woven branches plastered with mud and straw.

In the middle there was a fire for cooking and keeping warm. Smoke would drift up through the roof. Beds were benches piled with straw and animal skins.

IRON AGE LIVING

This reconstructed roundhouse is in Castell Henllys in Pembrokeshire. The walls and posts have been decorated with patterns. We don't know for sure if the Celts did this, but we know they loved patterns (see p24).

AROUND THE HOUSE

Cooking pots and containers made from wood, animal skin or pottery would be in the roundhouse. There might be a loom for weaving woollen fabric, and some stones used for grinding up grain to make flour. If they were lucky, a family might have an iron cauldron to hang over the fire for cooking. The width of a roundhouse varied from 5 m up to 15 m. Measure your biggest room at home to see how it compares.

IRON AGE DINNER

Celts gathered food from the countryside and ate it with meat from their farm animals. They baked bread in a homemade clay oven and then dipped it in food (they didn't have cutlery). Chiefs had the biggest roundhouses, and sometimes threw feasts for their supporters. Here is an imaginary everyday menu based on what we know Iron Age people ate:

- Porridge-like stew of vegetables, grain and meat.
- Flatbread made with wheat and barley flour.
- Soft curd cheese.
- Wild honey and fruits from the forest.

▲ Later in the Iron Age Celtic chiefs got a taste for luxury. The tall Roman wine pots at the back of this picture come from a chieftain's grave in Hertfordshire.

DID CELTS HAVE TOILETS?

No. They went outside, in a hole in the ground, and probably used moss to wipe themselves.

MEET THE FAMILY

We don't know very much about individual Iron Age people or family life, but we can work out some things from Roman writing and from the objects found in graves.

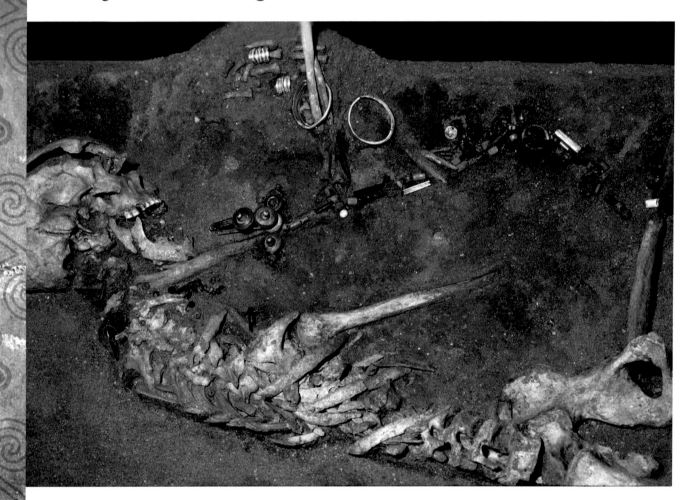

SKELETON STATS

From studies of Iron Age bones we know that Celtic women were, on average, 1.57 m tall and men were, on average, 1.69 m tall. Life expectancy (the number

▲ This person was buried with treasures such as jewellery.

of years someone lives) was around 35 (50 years at most). Many children died young.

FAMILY LIFE

Roman leader Julius Caesar mentioned that some Celtic women had several husbands, though we've no idea if that was normal. We do know that Celtic women had more rights and power than Roman women. According to Caesar, the children of important Celts were often sent to live with relatives. This was probably done to strengthen family links and loyalty.

WHEN SOMEONE DIED

Iron Age people who were buried were given objects to take with them to an afterlife. Chiefs and important warriors were buried with many things, even whole carts and horses. Ordinary people who weren't cremated were laid to rest with just a few things that were important to them, such as a bead necklace or a tool. Many Iron Age people were not buried, though.

WHAT WERE CELTS CALLED?

The local British names we know of were mostly written down in the time after the Iron Age, when the Romans ruled. However, the same names might well have been used in the Iron Age, too. Here are a few of the shortest ones.

Girls: **Banna, Cata, Enica, Lucile, Ria, Senna.**

Boys: **Atto, Bel, Bri, Con, Luti, Tamm**

FROM THE IRON AGE

Boars were a symbol of war, and little boar figurines, such as the one on the right, were sometimes buried with warriors. It seems that boars were seen as magical creatures of the gods who brought luck and protection, even for a dead person when they went to an afterlife.

WHAT DID CELTS LOOK LIKE?

Roman visitors to Britain described what the Iron Age Celts looked like. Some jewellery and fragments of Iron Age clothing have been found, too.

This picture of an Iron Age Celtic man comes from the side of a decorated cart found in a grave. He has a lovely big moustache! ▶

HAIRY AND BLUE

When Roman leader Julius Caesar arrived he said that the southern Britons he met were all painted blue! They may have used juice from a plant called woad to colour their skin before a battle. Woad is a very good antiseptic and helps to heal wounds, so it sounds like a good idea. Caesar said that all the Celts had long hair and the men had long moustaches (Romans liked to be clean-shaven themselves). Here's a translation of what one Roman writer wrote about the Celts' moustaches:

'When they are eating, the moustache gets entangled in the food, and when they are drinking the drink gets sieved through it.'

CHECKS AND CLOAKS

Celtic men wore close-fitting trousers called braccae and a woolly tunic with a belt. The women wore a simple tube-

14

FROM THE IRON AGE

This beautiful Iron Age gold jewellery was found near Winchester, Hampshire. There were neck rings called torcs, bracelets and brooches.

The collection would have been an unusual and precious possession in Iron Age times. Perhaps a chieftain owned it.

The largest piece shown is a torc, worn round the neck. ▼

shaped long dress. When it was cold everyone wore cloaks pinned with brooches. The Celts dressed colourfully. They used plants to dye clothing brown, yellow, blue and red, and they liked to wear plaid - a pattern of squares rather like tartan.

HOME-MADE MAKE-UP

Later on in the Iron Age a few people may have worn make-up. 2,000 year-old grinding tools have been found that were used to grind up minerals (stones) into powder for eye shadow or face colouring.

WHAT WAS CELTIC HAIR LIKE?

Men and women wore their hair long, sometimes in plaits. Some Celtic coins show men with spiky hair, too. Iron Age hair gel made from plant resin was found on one Iron Age body preserved in a bog in Ireland.

MEET THE MAKERS

Some Iron Age Celts were skilled workers who could make swords and tools, pottery or woodwork.

METAL MAKERS

To make iron took skill, and only a few people could do it. First they made charcoal by burning wood. Then they built a clay furnace shaped like a chimney. They packed the charcoal into the furnace along with iron ore – iron found in stones dug from the ground. The hot charcoal melted the iron, which then ran out of the ore. The pure iron could be beaten into a shape such as a tool or a sword by a blacksmith or swordsmith.

FINDING THE CRAFTSPEOPLE

Sometimes craftspeople were buried with their craft tools. For instance, at Rudston in Yorkshire an Iron Age man was buried with a pair of blacksmith's tongs and a hammer, as well as a short sword and some spearheads. We can make a good guess that he was the blacksmith who made them. Weaving tools are often found in the graves of Iron Age women. They were probably the most skilled weavers of the time.

◀ Iron Age metalworkers were good artists. Whoever made this lovely little bronze horse's head was imaginative and skilled. It comes from Stanwick in Yorkshire, and may once have decorated a container.

This little tool is a weaving comb used when weaving woollen cloth on a loom. The Iron Age owner probably hung it by a cord from her belt. It was found in a hill fort at Ham Hill, Somerset.

This weaving comb is made of animal bone and decorated with carved lines. ▼

INDUSTRY BEGINS

When something is made on a big scale we call it an industry. One of the first industries in Britain was Iron Age salt-making. At sites we call salt works, on the east coast of England, Iron Age workers evaporated (boiled away) seawater over fires to get the sea salt left behind. Pots of salt were then sent to other parts of the country or even abroad. Salt preserved food and kept it from rotting over the winter.

WHO MADE THE MOST MONEY IN IRON AGE TIMES?

The richest people were the tribal chiefs and their warriors, not ordinary craftspeople or farmers. Towards the end of the Iron Age we know that chiefs were paying their warriors with gold coins.

SELLING BY SEA

Towards the end of the Iron Age there were lots more visitors to Britain and more trade with the rest of Europe. We know that the most powerful Celts became wealthy by selling goods abroad and using their wealth to buy luxuries.

BOATS FROM BRITAIN

It would have been hard to travel along the muddy tracks of Iron Age Britain. It was easier to carry goods in wooden boats, by river or along the coast. We know that Hengistbury in Dorset was a busy Late Iron Age port where boats arrived or set sail for Europe and smaller boats came by river from other parts of the country, carrying goods to sell. Britain was known in Europe for its wheat, wool and metals, but also for fine hunting dogs - big shaggy dogs that looked rather like modern Irish wolfhounds.

This very rare 10m-long Iron Age boat was carved from an oak log around 295 BCE. It was found in Poole Harbour, Dorset. Archaeologists have managed to preserve it by soaking it in sugar syrup for five years. ▼

SLAVES FOR SALE

Slaves were chained together by their necks and shipped to Europe on board Late Iron Age boats. British slaves were highly-prized abroad, and selling them helped make tribal chiefs wealthy. The slaves were probably people captured from enemy tribes. A lake in North Wales has revealed a chilling find - an Iron Age slave chain with five small neck rings, perhaps for children.

LUXURY LIVING

Around 50 BCE members of the Atrebates tribe were living in one of Britain's first towns, now called Silchester in Hampshire. They were no longer poor farming folk. Now they had luxury imports such as olive oil, wine and spices from Italy, and fashionable pottery from Germany and France. In return they were selling something rather surprising. Archaeologists found lots of skinned puppy bones and think it might be evidence of a puppy-fur cloak industry.

FROM THE IRON AGE

This heavy iron slave chain was once thrown into a Welsh lake, perhaps as an offering to Celtic gods.

The rings are sized to fit the necks of small slaves. ▼

WHAT ELSE DID THE CELTS GET FROM ABROAD?

Towards the end of the Iron Age wealthy Britons began eating from plates for the first time. It was a fashion that probably came from France. They must have thought they were very sophisticated!

19

MEDICINE WITH MAGIC

If you became ill you would be given medicines made from plants and herbs. The best healing experts were probably the Druid priests and priestesses. They may have performed magic rituals on their patients as well as giving them cures.

THE DOCTOR'S GRAVE

A grave found in Stanway, Essex, is thought to be the resting place of a doctor-Druid healer from the Late Iron Age. The doctor was buried with some of the oldest surgical instruments found in Britain so far – including forceps, a scalpel, a surgical saw and a stitching needle. These would have been used during operations, perhaps to help mend broken bones or battle wounds.

REMEDIES

Plants were used to make healing drinks. The doctor-Druid was buried along with a tea-strainer that still contained the remains of herbs used to make herbal tea. Plants were also mixed with animal fat, tree resin or honey to make ointments. Powdered minerals were used, too. Divers exploring an Iron Age shipwreck near Italy found a tin of tiny pills containing the metal, zinc. It's possible the pills may have been ground into a paste to use for skin complaints. Zinc is still used in skin creams today.

ADDED MAGIC

In the doctor-Druid's grave there were eight mysterious metal rods. It's thought they might be divining rods, which could have

WHAT ILLNESSES DID IRON AGE PEOPLE HAVE?

We can tell some illnesses from bones, so we know that Iron Age people often suffered from arthritis, and sometimes malnutrition (not enough to eat).

been used in a special ceremony to predict future events. Perhaps the doctor-Druid used them to decide on the best time to perform an operation. We can only guess because nobody ever wrote about them. In the grave there was also a bead made from jet – a rare type of shiny black stone. Jet was probably thought to have magical powers in Iron Age times.

FROM THE IRON AGE

As well as medical equipment the doctor-Druid was buried with a board game, with two different coloured sets of glass counters. Perhaps the doctor just liked games, or perhaps the counters were used in some kind of magical prediction ceremony.

▼ An archaeologist holds some of the tools and rods found in the doctor-Druid's grave.

PLEASING THE GODS

The Celts believed in many gods and goddesses. They held festivals and mysterious rituals to try to please them and sometimes even offered them human sacrifices. The Druids probably led the rituals.

SACRED WATER

Valuable Celtic treasures such as swords, shields and cauldrons were sometimes thrown into rivers and lakes. The Celts probably thought that the water was a way into a magical otherworld where their gods and goddesses lived. They may have thrown in the best things they owned as offerings.

This bronze shield was thrown into the River Thames as an offering. ▼

MURDERED!

Lindow Man was sacrificed 2,000 years ago (you can see him on p5). His body was discovered preserved in a dried-up peat bog at Lindow Moss in Cheshire. He was knocked out, strangled and pushed into the bog. Other sacrificed humans have been found in bogs around northern Europe, possibly killed as offerings to the gods.

WHAT WOULD IT BE LIKE TO GO TO A CELTIC FESTIVAL?

Everyone would gather together for feasting and perhaps dancing and music (the Celts had drums, flutes and horns). There would probably be bonfires and perhaps a Druid altar for animal sacrifices.

FROM THE IRON AGE

This panel is part of the silver Gundestrup Cauldron, thrown into a Danish bog in Iron Age times. It's thought that the picture may show somebody being sacrificed, possibly being drowned in a container of liquid.

A YEAR OF FESTIVALS

The Celts celebrated festivals based on the changing of the seasons. They held feasts and religious ceremonies to please their gods and goddesses and ensure a good farming year. If the gods were angry they might send bad weather. Without a good harvest, everyone would go hungry.

ART AND STORIES

The Iron Age wasn't all about fighting and farming. Celtic craftspeople of the time made some beautiful objects, finely decorated with patterns. There was spoken poetry and music, too.

▲ This is part of the Battersea Shield, thrown into the River Thames in Iron Age times. Can you see an owl-like face in the decoration? Celtic designs often had animal and human faces hidden in them.

SWIRLY STYLE

Valuable objects, such as weapons and jewellery, were decorated with swirls and spirals that look rather like plant tendrils. The interlocking patterns sometimes had animals or human heads incorporated into them, too. We call this style of decoration 'La Tène', after a place in Switzerland where lots of Iron Age objects were found.

SINGING OUT STORIES

Some Celts were bards, which means they told tales in poetry and song. Chieftains had their own personal bards to entertain them. As they sang, the bards plucked the strings of an instrument, like a harp-player does today. A wooden fragment of a Celtic musical instrument turned up on Skye in the Western Isles of Scotland. It was

FROM THE IRON AGE

This beautiful bronze mirror was found in Desborough, Northamptonshire. The back has been decorated with lots of swirls, typical of the Iron Age. Several finely-made mirrors like this have been found in the graves of British Iron Age women.

This mirror would have been a rare and costly object. ▶

an incredibly rare find dating from 2,300 years ago, making it the oldest stringed instrument ever found in the whole of western Europe.

MYTHS AND MAGIC

The bards would probably have told tales of battle victories, gods and goddesses. We don't know what the stories were, but we can guess from looking at Celtic carving that there were myths about monsters, warriors and magical creatures. Iron Age people didn't just think of magic as part of a story, though. They believed in magic for real.

WHAT LANGUAGE DID THE CELTS SPEAK?

Iron Age Celts spoke a language we wouldn't understand. We still have a few place names from Celtic times, though, especially the names of rivers. The Thames, the Avon, the Derwent, the Stour and the Wye are examples. Perhaps later people thought it would be unlucky to change river names because they were once connected to ancient gods and goddesses.

HERE COME THE ROMANS

Life began to change for some people in Iron Age Britain when new rulers arrived. The ancient Romans took control of the southern part of Britain - around 2,000 years ago.

NEW INVADERS

Julius Caesar brought a fleet of Roman ships to Britain in 55 BCE. When they arrived, the Roman soldiers saw Celtic warriors massed on the cliffs of Dover ready to fight them. Storms made it hard for Caesar to land his troops, but he returned the next year to try again. The Celtic tribes' resistance became disorganised, making things easier for Caesar. Some of them made an agreement with him. He imposed a yearly tax payment on them and went home to Rome. Meanwhile not much changed for ordinary Celts.

BACK FOR GOOD

The Romans returned in CE 43, this time to take more control. Some tribes fought back and were smashed. Others worked with the Romans, promising loyalty in return for local power.

The conquering Roman Emperor Claudius arrived in Colchester and got a promise of loyalty from eleven tribal leaders. This time the fate of ordinary people depended on their leaders. Some died fighting. Others ended up working for the Romans.

CHIEF IN A PALACE

One tribal chief called Cogidubnus became very powerful by helping the Roman conquerers. It's thought he might

WHY DID THE ROMANS COME?

The Romans wanted Britain's metals, such as lead and silver. They also wanted to stop local tribes from making trouble for their empire.

have lived in Fishbourne Palace, a luxury Roman-style residence near Chichester. If that's true, he had come a long way from Iron Age life. Now he had a mansion with a hundred rooms, fine mosaics, underfloor heating and a beautiful garden. We know he took a Roman name - Tiberius Claudius Cogidubnus. He was no longer an Iron Age leader. He was a Romano-British leader - someone from Britain who lived in Roman style. He had left behind crowded roundhouses and mud floors!

FROM THE IRON AGE ? NO!

Cogidubnus may even have lived in Rome as a young man, and would have had a taste for Roman fashions. This Fishbourne Palace floor shows a fine Roman mosaic of the Roman god Cupid riding on a dolphin.

Craftsmen from abroad probably came to Britain to make this mosaic. ▼

WHAT HAPPENED TO THE CELTS?

It took 90 years for the Romans to get full control of England and Wales. Scotland and Ireland were never conquered, and Celtic life continued there.

◀ This giant figure is at the Green Man Music Festival, held every year in Wales. The green man is a figure from ancient legend, possibly based on a powerful Celtic horned god of nature called Cernunnos.

DEATH TO THE DRUIDS

We know that the Romans had fierce battles with some Celtic tribes hiding in their hill forts. They also had to contend with surprise ambushes from small bands of Celts as they marched through the countryside. There was violent rebellion and the Romans blamed the Druids for stirring things up. In CE 60 they marched on Anglesey in Wales, the stronghold of the Druids, smashing their altars and killing their priests and priestesses.

PEACE AT LAST

Gradually the tribes of southern Britain were put under Roman control. Many people eventually began to do things the Roman

way, worshipping Roman gods, wearing Roman clothes and eating Roman-style food. It didn't happen to everyone, though. In Scotland and Ireland people kept their tribal traditions and ancient way of living.

STORIES AND SWIRLS STAY

The Romans ruled in southern Britain for 400 years, and the Iron Age way of life began to disappear there. Celtic culture lived on in Scotland and Ireland, where people still created the swirly patterned art style that began in the Iron Age. Magical mysterious stories survived from the Iron Age, too. Some of Britain and Ireland's most ancient legends probably come from that long-gone time.

GLOSSARY

Afterlife The idea of a new life in a heavenly place, after death on Earth.

Archaeologist An expert who studies human objects and remains from the past.

Arthritis A disease that causes stiff and painful joints.

Bard A singing poet.

Braccae Woollen trousers worn in Iron Age times.

Community A group of people.

Crannog A thatched round hut built on a platform over a lake.

Cremated When a body is burnt after death.

Divining rod A rod used to make magical predictions.

Druids Iron Age priests and priestesses.

Forceps A pair of tweezers or pincers used during surgery.

Furnace A container for heating materials to a very high temperature.

Hill fort A settlement of Iron Age homes on top of a hill, surrounded by ditches and banks.

Imports Products brought in from abroad.

La Tène A type of swirly art style used in Iron Age times.

Life expectancy How long people live.

Loom Equipment for making fabric by weaving woollen thread.

Malnutrition When someone has eaten so little they become ill.

Oppidum A big settlement of Iron Age homes laid out along streets.

Plaid A checked pattern on fabric.

Population The number of people in a country or settlement.

Resin A sticky substance from trees.

Predictions Suggestions about what will happen in the future.

Ritual A ceremony repeated the same way over and over again.

Romano-British A Briton who lived under the rule of the ancient Romans.

Roundhouse A round hut with a pointed thatched roof.

Sacrifice Giving something up. In the Iron Age people sacrificed objects and humans to their gods.

Torc A neck ring worn as jewellery.

Woad A plant used to make blue dye.

SOME IRON AGE WEBSITES

A map showing the approximate location of Celtic Iron Age tribes in Britain:
www.bbc.co.uk/history/ancient/british_prehistory/iron_01.shtml

See inside reconstructed Iron Age longhouses in Wales:
http://resourcesforhistory.com/Celtic_round_houses.htm#gsc.tab=0

From the BBC: How did Iron Age people live?:
www.bbc.co.uk/guides/z8bkwmn

Build a virtual roundhouse and step inside:
http://tastesofhistory.blogspot.com/2018/03/one-pot-cooking.html

Note to parents and teachers: Every effort has been made by the Publishers to ensure that the web sites in this book are suitable for children, that they are of the highest educational value, and that they contain no inappropriate or offensive material. However, because of the nature of the Internet, it is impossible to guarantee that the contents of these sites will not be altered. We strongly advise that Internet access is supervised by a responsible adult.

TIMELINE

800 BCE Iron-making spread to Britain, and the period we call the Iron Age began (replacing the Bronze Age).

700 BCE The first hill forts were built.

500-100 BCE The biggest hill forts were built, and the brochs in Scotland.

330 BCE Greek explorer Pytheas sailed round Britain and became the first person to describe the people who lived in Britain.

300 BCE Celtic craftsmen began to decorate objects with swirling patterns.

100 BCE Coins were used for the first time, but only in the southeast of England.

55 BCE Ancient Roman troops arrived in Britain for the first time, under Julius Caesar.

50 BCE The Atrebates tribe were living in one of Britain's first towns, in Silchester, Hants.

CE 43 The ancient Romans returned to conquer southern Britain and Wales (not Scotland or Ireland).

CE 60 The Roman army attacked the Druid stronghold of Anglesey, Wales, and destroyed the Druid stronghold there.

INDEX